FAVORITE BRAND NAME™

NEW

Diabetic
RECIPES

Publications International, Ltd.

Favorite Brand Name Recipes at www.fbnr.com

Nutritional Analysis: Linda R. Yoakam, M.S., R.D., L.D.

Pictured on the front cover *(clockwise from right):* Chicken Piccata *(page 40),* Gingered Chicken with Vegetables *(page 44),* Nutmeg Pancakes with Lemon-Spiked Berries *(page 20)* and Ginger Shrimp Salad *(page 76).*

Pictured on the back cover *(clockwise from top):* Italian-Style Meat Loaf *(page 24),* Baked Pear Dessert *(page 78),* Tangy Apple Slaw *(page 68)* and Chicken with Spinach and Celery Hash *(page 56).*

Nutritional Analysis: The nutritional information that appears with each recipe was submitted in part by the participating companies and associations. Every effort has been made to check the accuracy of these numbers. However, because numerous variables account for a wide range of values for certain foods, nutritive analyses in this book should be considered approximate.

Microwave Cooking: Microwave ovens vary in wattage. Use the cooking times as guidelines and check for doneness before adding more time.

Preparation/Cooking Times: Preparation times are based on the approximate amount of time required to assemble the recipe before cooking, baking, chilling or serving. These times include preparation steps such as measuring, chopping and mixing. The fact that some preparations and cooking can be done simultaneously is taken into account. Preparation of optional ingredients and serving suggestions is not included.

table of
contents

introduction

Whether you or someone close to you has recently been diagnosed with diabetes or has been living with it for years, don't be discouraged. We now know more about diabetes than ever before, and research is constantly providing us with information on new and better ways of managing it. Today people with diabetes are living long, happy and healthy lives.

No Foods Are Forbidden

In the past, people with diabetes were told to monitor the amount of sugar in every food they ate. While it used to be thought that simple sugar, such as the type in cake and cookies, caused a larger rise in blood glucose than other types of carbohydrates, research has proven otherwise. Today the focus has shifted away from sugar to focus on the total amount of carbohydrates consumed throughout the day. Better known as "Carbohydrate Counting," this system is much more flexible than the older, more rigid Exchange System.

Instead of telling patients what foods to avoid, health professionals are now instructing them on healthy eating and what foods to choose. Registered dietitians and certified diabetes educators everywhere are working with patients, instructing them on ways to include a wide variety of foods—even sugary ones in moderation—in their meal plans. Because this system, "Carbohydrate Counting," is the one being taught by so many professionals today, the amount of sugar is not included with the nutritional analyses for the recipes in this book. You will, however, find the total amount of carbohydrates and the exchange information given for each recipe.

If you haven't already, ask your medical doctor or endocrinologist to refer you to a registered dietitian or a certified diabetes educator. Either of these professionals will talk with you and help you better understand your diabetes and instruct you on ways to control it. They will be able to calculate the number of servings of carbohydrates you need each day and can work with you to devise a meal plan that best fits your lifestyle.

It's All About Balance

Goals for healthful eating are based on total foods consumed throughout the day or over a period of time, instead of only on individual foods. A food might be high in carbohydrates, but if other foods eaten throughout the day are adjusted to meet a person's total suggested carbohydrate intake, the single high-carbohydrate food will not likely pose a problem. Because of this, a range of healthful recipes are included within this book. Some of the recipes are higher in sodium; some are higher in fat; and some are higher in carbohydrates or cholesterol. Moderation, portion sizes and planning are keys to success with any healthful eating plan.

A diagnosis of diabetes brings about a whole new way of living. The satisfying recipes in this book are intended to help make this transition as smooth as possible. Let them be your guide to providing delicious and nutritious meals!

country
breakfasts

Mini Vegetable Quiches

Makes 8 servings

- **2 cups cut-up vegetables (bell peppers, broccoli, zucchini and/or carrots)**
- **2 tablespoons chopped green onions**
- **2 tablespoons FLEISCHMANN'S® Original Margarine**
- **4 (8-inch) flour tortillas, each cut into 8 triangles**
- **1 cup EGG BEATERS®**
- **1 cup fat-free (skim) milk**
- **½ teaspoon dried basil leaves**

In medium nonstick skillet, over medium-high heat, sauté vegetables and green onions in margarine until tender.

Arrange 4 tortilla pieces in each of 8 (6-ounce) greased custard cups or ramekins, placing points of tortilla pieces at center of bottom of each cup and pressing lightly to form shape of cup. Divide vegetable mixture evenly among cups. In small bowl, combine Egg Beaters®, milk and basil. Pour evenly over vegetable mixture. Place cups on baking sheet. Bake at 375°F for 20 to 25 minutes or until puffed and knife inserted into centers comes out clean. Let stand 5 minutes before serving.

Nutrients per serving: 1 Quiche
Calories: 115, **Calories from Fat:** 30%, **Total Fat:** 4g,
Saturated Fat: 1g, **Cholesterol:** 1mg, **Sodium:** 184mg,
Carbohydrate: 14g, **Fiber:** 1g, **Protein:** 6g

Dietary Exchange: ½ Starch, 2 Vegetable, ½ Fat

Mini Vegetable Quiches

Eggs Benedict

Makes 4 servings

        Mock Hollandaise Sauce (recipe follows)
    4   **eggs, divided**
    2   **English muffins, halved**
        Fresh spinach leaves, washed and drained
    8   **ounces sliced lean Canadian bacon**
    4   **tomato slices, cut ¼ inch thick**
        Paprika

1. Prepare Mock Hollandaise Sauce. Set aside.

2. Bring 6 cups water to a boil in large saucepan over high heat. Reduce heat to simmer. Carefully break 1 egg into small dish and slide egg into water. Repeat with remaining 3 eggs. Simmer, uncovered, about 5 minutes or until yolks are just set.

3. Meanwhile, toast muffin halves; place on serving plates. Top each muffin half with spinach leaves, 2 ounces Canadian bacon, 1 tomato slice and 1 egg. Spoon 3 tablespoons Mock Hollandaise Sauce over egg; sprinkle with paprika. Serve with fresh fruit, if desired.

Mock Hollandaise Sauce: Process 4 ounces fat-free cream cheese, 3 tablespoons plain nonfat yogurt, 1 tablespoon lemon juice and 1 tablespoon Dijon mustard in food processor or blender until smooth. Heat in small saucepan over medium-high heat until hot. Makes ¾ cup sauce.

Note: Select only clean, fresh eggs from refrigerated display cases. Don't use dirty, cracked or leaking eggs. When cracking eggs, avoid getting any shell in with the raw eggs. Be sure to wash your hands, utensils and countertops after working with eggs.

Nutrients per serving: 1 muffin half with 3 to 4 spinach leaves, 2 ounces Canadian bacon, 1 tomato slice, 1 egg and 3 tablespoons sauce
Calories: 237, **Calories from Fat:** 25%, **Total Fat:** 6g,
Saturated Fat: 2g, **Cholesterol:** 248mg, **Sodium:** 1,209mg,
Carbohydrate: 19g, **Fiber:** 1g, **Protein:** 24g

Dietary Exchange: 1 Starch, ½ Vegetable, 2½ Meat

Eggs Benedict

Easy Raspberry-Peach Danish
Makes 32 servings (2 coffee cakes)

   1 loaf (16 ounces) frozen white bread dough, thawed
   ⅓ cup all-fruit raspberry spread
   1 can (16 ounces) sliced peaches in juice, drained and
       chopped
   1 egg white, beaten (optional)
   ½ cup powdered sugar
   2 to 3 teaspoons orange juice
   ¼ cup chopped pecans, toasted

1. Preheat oven to 350°F. Spray 2 baking sheets with nonstick cooking spray.

2. Place dough on lightly floured surface. Cut dough in half. Roll each half into 12×7-inch rectangle. Place 1 rectangle on each prepared baking sheet.

3. Spread half of raspberry spread over center third of each dough rectangle. Sprinkle peaches over raspberry spread. On both long sides of each dough rectangle, make 2-inch long cuts from edges towards filling at 1-inch intervals. Starting at one end, alternately fold opposite strips of dough over filling.

4. Cover; let rise in warm place about 1 hour or until nearly doubled in size. Bake 15 to 20 minutes or until golden. If deeper golden color is desired, lightly brush egg white over tops of coffee cakes during last 5 minutes of baking. Remove coffee cakes from baking sheet. Cool slightly.

5. Combine powdered sugar and enough orange juice in small bowl until desired drizzling consistency is reached. Drizzle over both coffee cakes. Sprinkle with pecans. Cut each coffee cake into 16 slices.

Prep Time: 15 minutes
Rising Time: 1 hour
Bake Time: 15 to 20 minutes

Nutrients per serving: 2 slices
Calories: 145, **Calories from Fat:** 15%, **Total Fat:** 2g,
Saturated Fat: <1g, **Cholesterol:** 0mg, **Sodium:** 240mg,
Carbohydrate: 26g, **Fiber:** 2g, **Protein:** 4g

Dietary Exchange: 1 Starch, 1 Fruit, ½ Fat

Easy Raspberry-Peach Danish

Farmstand Frittata

Makes 4 servings

Nonstick cooking spray
½ cup chopped onion
1 medium red bell pepper, seeded and cut into thin strips
1 cup broccoli florets, blanched and drained
1 cup cooked, quartered unpeeled red potatoes
1 cup cholesterol-free egg substitute
6 egg whites
1 tablespoon chopped fresh parsley
½ teaspoon salt
¼ teaspoon black pepper
½ cup (2 ounces) shredded reduced-fat Cheddar cheese

1. Spray large nonstick ovenproof skillet with cooking spray; heat over medium heat until hot. Add onion and bell pepper; cook and stir 3 minutes or until crisp-tender.

2. Add broccoli and potatoes; cook and stir 1 to 2 minutes or until heated through.

3. Whisk together egg substitute, egg whites, parsley, salt and black pepper in medium bowl.

4. Spread vegetables into even layer in skillet. Pour egg white mixture over vegetables; cover and cook over medium heat 10 to 12 minutes or until egg mixture is set.

5. Meanwhile, preheat broiler. Top frittata with cheese. Broil 4 inches from heat 1 minute or until cheese is melted. Cut into four wedges.

Nutrients per serving: 1 Frittata wedge (¼ of total recipe)
Calories: 163, **Calories from Fat:** 12%, **Total Fat:** 2g,
Saturated Fat: 1g, **Cholesterol:** 8mg, **Sodium:** 686mg,
Carbohydrate: 19g, **Fiber:** 2g, **Protein:** 17g

Dietary Exchange: 1 Starch, 2 Meat

Farmstand Frittata

Western Omelet

Makes 2 servings

- ½ **cup finely chopped red or green bell pepper**
- ⅓ **cup cubed cooked potato**
- 2 **slices turkey bacon, diced**
- ¼ **teaspoon dried oregano leaves**
- 2 **teaspoons FLEISCHMANN'S® Original Margarine, divided**
- 1 **cup EGG BEATERS®**
- **Fresh oregano sprig, for garnish**

In 8-inch nonstick skillet over medium heat sauté bell pepper, potato, turkey bacon and dried oregano in 1 teaspoon margarine until tender. Remove from skillet; keep warm.

In same skillet, over medium heat, melt remaining 1 teaspoon margarine. Pour Egg Beaters® into skillet. Cook, lifting edges to allow uncooked portion to flow underneath. When almost set, spoon vegetable mixture over half of omelet. Fold other half over vegetable mixture; slide onto serving plate. Garnish with fresh oregano.

Prep Time: 15 minutes
Cook Time: 10 minutes

Note: For a frittata, sauté vegetables, turkey bacon and dried oregano in 2 teaspoons margarine. Pour Egg Beaters® evenly into skillet over vegetable mixture. Cook without stirring for 4 to 5 minutes or until cooked on bottom and almost set on top. Carefully turn frittata; cook for 1 to 2 minutes more or until done. Slide onto serving platter; cut into wedges to serve.

Nutrients per serving: ½ of omelet (without fruit)
Calories: 166, **Calories from Fat:** 30%, **Total Fat:** 6g,
Saturated Fat: 1g, **Cholesterol:** 10mg, **Sodium:** 423mg,
Carbohydrate: 14g, **Fiber:** 2g, **Protein:** 15g

Dietary Exchange: 1 Starch, 2 Meat

Western Omelet

Strawberry Cinnamon French Toast

Makes 4 servings

- 1 egg
- ¼ cup fat-free (skim) milk
- ½ teaspoon vanilla
- 4 (1-inch-thick) diagonally cut slices Italian bread (about 1 ounce each)
- 2 teaspoons reduced-fat margarine
- 2 packets sugar substitute
- ¼ teaspoon ground cinnamon
- 1 cup sliced strawberries
  Fresh mint leaves, for garnish (optional)

1. Preheat oven to 450°F.

2. Spray nonstick baking sheet with nonstick cooking spray; set aside.

3. Beat egg, milk and vanilla in shallow dish or pie plate until blended. Dip bread slices in egg mixture until completely coated and all egg mixture is absorbed. Place on baking sheet; bake 15 minutes or until golden, turning over halfway through baking time.

4. Meanwhile, combine margarine, sugar substitute and cinnamon in small bowl; stir until well blended. Spread mixture evenly over French toast. Top with strawberries. Garnish with mint, if desired.

Prep Time: 10 minutes
Bake Time: 15 minutes

Nutrients per serving: 1 French toast slice with ¼ cup strawberries
Calories: 125, **Calories from Fat:** 23%, **Total Fat:** 3g,
Saturated Fat: 1g, **Cholesterol:** 53mg, **Sodium:** 220mg,
Carbohydrate: 19g, **Fiber:** 2g, **Protein:** 5g

Dietary Exchange: 1 Starch, ½ Fat

Strawberry Cinnamon French Toast

Nutmeg Pancakes with Lemon-Spiked Berries

Makes 6 servings

- 1 cup all-purpose flour
- 2 tablespoons granular sucralose-based sugar substitute, divided
- 1 teaspoon baking powder
- ¾ teaspoon ground nutmeg
- ½ teaspoon baking soda
- ¼ teaspoon salt
- 1⅓ cups nonfat buttermilk
- ¼ cup cholesterol-free egg substitute
- 2 tablespoons canola oil
- 2 cups sliced strawberries
- 2 teaspoons finely grated lemon peel

1. Combine flour, 1 tablespoon sugar substitute, baking powder, nutmeg, baking soda and salt in small bowl. Combine buttermilk, egg substitute and oil In another small bowl. Add to flour mixture; stir just until moistened.

2. Lightly spray nonstick griddle with nonstick cooking spray. Heat over medium-high heat. For each pancake, pour about ¼ cup batter onto hot griddle. Cook until top is covered with bubbles and edge is slightly dry. Turn; continue cooking until done.

3. Meanwhile, combine strawberries, remaining 1 tablespoon sugar substitute and lemon peel in medium bowl. Serve berries over warm pancakes.

Prep Time: 10 minutes
Cook Time: 3 to 4 minutes

Nutrients per serving: 1 pancake with ⅓ cup strawberry mixture
Calories: 162, **Calories from Fat:** 30%, **Total Fat:** 5g,
Saturated Fat: 1g, **Cholesterol:** 2mg, **Sodium:** 361mg,
Carbohydrate: 23g, **Fiber:** 2g, **Protein:** 5g

Dietary Exchange: 1 Starch, 1 Fruit, 1 Fat

Nutmeg Pancakes with Lemon-Spiked Berries

sunday dinners

Chicken with Orange Almond Sauce

Makes 4 servings

Butter-flavored cooking spray
4 (4 ounces each) skinless boneless chicken breast halves
1 cup orange juice
⅓ cup SPLENDA® No Calorie Sweetener, Granular
2 tablespoons cornstarch
1 can (11 ounces) mandarin oranges, rinsed and drained
2 tablespoons slivered almonds
1 teaspoon dried onion flakes
1 teaspoon dried parsley flakes

1. In large skillet sprayed with cooking spray, brown chicken pieces for 4 to 5 minutes on each side.

2. Meanwhile, in covered jar, combine orange juice, SPLENDA® and cornstarch. Shake well to blend.

3. Pour sauce mixture into medium saucepan sprayed with cooking spray. Cook over medium heat until mixture thickens, stirring constantly. Remove from heat.

4. Stir mandarin oranges, almonds, onion flakes and parsley flakes into sauce. Spoon sauce evenly over browned chicken breasts.

5. Reduce heat and simmer for 5 minutes or until chicken is no longer pink in center. When serving, evenly spoon sauce over chicken breasts.

Nutrients per serving: ¼ of total recipe
Calories: 188, **Calories from Fat:** 16%, **Total Fat:** 3g,
Saturated Fat: <1g, **Cholesterol:** 43mg, **Sodium:** 47mg,
Carbohydrate: 21g, **Fiber:** 1g, **Protein:** 19g
Dietary Exchange: 1 Fruit, 2½ Meat

Chicken with Orange Almond Sauce

Italian-Style Meat Loaf

Makes 8 servings

        1 can (6 ounces) no-salt-added tomato paste
        ½ cup dry red wine plus ½ cup water *or* 1 cup water
        1 teaspoon minced garlic
        ½ teaspoon dried basil leaves
        ½ teaspoon dried oregano leaves
        ¼ teaspoon salt
        ¾ pound 95% lean ground beef
        ¾ pound 93% lean ground turkey breast
        1 cup fresh whole wheat bread crumbs (2 slices whole wheat
              bread)
        ½ cup shredded zucchini
        ¼ cup cholesterol-free egg substitute *or* 2 egg whites

1. Preheat oven to 350°F. Combine tomato paste, wine, water, garlic, basil, oregano and salt in small saucepan. Bring to a boil; reduce heat to low. Simmer, uncovered, 15 minutes. Set aside.

2. Combine beef, turkey, bread crumbs, zucchini, egg substitute and ½ cup reserved tomato paste mixture in large bowl. Mix well. Shape into loaf; place in ungreased 9×5-inch loaf pan. Bake 45 minutes. Discard any drippings. Pour remaining tomato paste mixture over top of loaf. Bake 15 minutes more or until juices run clear (160°F in center). Place on serving platter. Cool 10 minutes before cutting into 8 slices. Garnish as desired.

Nutrients per serving: 1 slice (⅛ of meat loaf)
Calories: 187, **Calories from Fat:** 11%, **Total Fat:** 2g,
Saturated Fat: 1g, **Cholesterol:** 41mg, **Sodium:** 171mg,
Carbohydrate: 12g, **Fiber:** 1g, **Protein:** 19g

Dietary Exchange: 1 Starch, 2 Meat

Italian-Style Meat Loaf

Chicken Pot Pie

Makes 4 servings

- 2 **teaspoons margarine**
- ½ **cup plus 2 tablespoons fat-free reduced-sodium chicken broth, divided**
- 2 **cups sliced mushrooms**
- 1 **cup diced red bell pepper**
- ½ **cup chopped onion**
- ½ **cup chopped celery**
- 2 **tablespoons all-purpose flour**
- ½ **cup fat-free half-and-half**
- 2 **cups cubed cooked chicken breasts**
- 1 **teaspoon minced fresh dill**
- ½ **teaspoon salt**
- ¼ **teaspoon black pepper**
- 2 **reduced-fat refrigerated crescent rolls**

1. Heat margarine and 2 tablespoons chicken broth in medium saucepan until margarine is melted. Add mushrooms, bell pepper, onion and celery. Cook 7 to 10 minutes or until vegetables are tender, stirring frequently.

2. Stir in flour; cook 1 minute. Stir in remaining ½ cup chicken broth; cook and stir until liquid thickens. Reduce heat and stir in half-and-half. Add chicken, dill, salt and black pepper.

3. Preheat oven to 375°F. Spray 1-quart casserole with nonstick cooking spray. Spoon chicken mixture into prepared dish. Roll out crescent rolls and place on top of chicken mixture.*

4. Bake pot pie 20 minutes or until topping is golden and filling is bubbly.

Reserve remaining rolls for another use, or bake and serve as a side to Chicken Pot Pie.

Note: For 2 cups cubed cooked chicken breast, gently simmer 3 small skinless chicken breasts in 2 cups fat-free reduced-sodium chicken broth about 20 minutes or until meat is no longer pink in center. Cool and cut into cubes. Reserve chicken broth for pot pie, if desired.

Nutrients per serving: 1 cup pot pie
Calories: 256, **Calories from Fat:** 28%, **Total Fat:** 8g,
Saturated Fat: 2g, **Cholesterol:** 50mg, **Sodium:** 541mg,
Carbohydrate: 18g, **Fiber:** 2g, **Protein:** 24g

Dietary Exchange: 1 Starch, 1 Vegetable, 3 Meat

Chicken Pot Pie

Roast Turkey Breast with Apple-Corn Bread Stuffing

Makes 6 servings

	Nonstick cooking spray
1	medium onion, chopped
1¼	cups fat-free reduced-sodium chicken broth
1	package (8 ounces) corn bread stuffing mix
1	Granny Smith apple, diced
¾	teaspoon dried sage, divided
¾	teaspoon dried thyme leaves, divided
1	boneless turkey breast (1½ pounds)
1	teaspoon paprika
¼	teaspoon black pepper

1. Preheat oven to 450°F. Coat 1½-quart casserole with cooking spray; set aside. Coat large saucepan with cooking spray; heat over medium heat. Add onion; cook and stir 5 minutes. Add broth; bring to a simmer. Stir in stuffing mix, apple, ¼ teaspoon sage and ¼ teaspoon thyme. Transfer mixture to prepared casserole; set aside.

2. Coat shallow roasting pan with cooking spray. Place turkey breast in pan, skin side up; coat with cooking spray. Mix paprika, remaining ½ teaspoon sage, ½ teaspoon thyme and pepper in small bowl; sprinkle over turkey. Spray lightly with cooking spray.

3. Roast turkey 15 minutes. *Reduce oven temperature to 350°F.* Place stuffing in oven alongside turkey; roast 35 minutes or until internal temperature of turkey reaches 170°F when tested with meat thermometer inserted into thickest part of breast. Transfer turkey to cutting board; cover with foil and let stand 10 to 15 minutes before carving. (Internal temperature will rise 5° to 10°F during stand time.) Remove stuffing from oven; cover to keep warm. Carve turkey into thin slices; serve with stuffing.

Nutrients per serving: ⅙ of total recipe
Calories: 304, **Calories from Fat:** 8%, **Total Fat:** 3g,
Saturated Fat: 1g, **Cholesterol:** 75mg, **Sodium:** 580mg,
Carbohydrate: 34g, **Fiber:** 7g, **Protein:** 33g

Dietary Exchange: 2 Starch, 4 Meat

Roast Turkey Breast with Apple-Corn Bread Stuffing

Beef Stroganoff

Makes 6 servings

- 1 boneless beef top sirloin steak (about 1 pound)
- 1 large onion, cut lengthwise and thinly sliced
- ½ cup plain nonfat yogurt
- ½ cup reduced-fat sour cream
- 3 tablespoons chopped chives, divided
- 2 tablespoons all-purpose flour
- 1 tablespoon ketchup
- 2 teaspoons Dijon mustard
- ¼ teaspoon salt
- ⅛ teaspoon white pepper
- 1 teaspoon olive oil
- 6 ounces portobello or button mushrooms, sliced
- 3½ cups cooked wide noodles
- 12 ounces baby carrots, steamed

1. Cut beef in half lengthwise, then crosswise into ¼-inch slices; set aside.

2. Heat large nonstick skillet over low heat; add onion. Cover; cook, stirring occasionally, 10 minutes or until tender. Remove onion from skillet; set aside.

3. Combine yogurt, sour cream, 2 tablespoons chives, flour, ketchup, mustard, salt and pepper in small bowl; set aside.

4. Heat oil in skillet over medium-high heat. Add beef and mushrooms; cook and stir 3 to 4 minutes or until beef is lightly browned. Return onion to skillet. Reduce heat to low. Stir in yogurt mixture until well blended and slightly thickened, about 2 minutes. Serve with noodles and carrots. Garnish with remaining 1 tablespoon chives.

Nutrients per serving: ½ cup noodles with ½ cup beef mixture and ½ cup cooked carrots
Calories: 246, **Calories from Fat:** 27%, **Total Fat:** 7g, **Saturated Fat:** 3g, **Cholesterol:** 65mg, **Sodium:** 256mg, **Carbohydrate:** 23g, **Fiber:** 2g, **Protein:** 22g

Dietary Exchange: 1 Starch, 1 Vegetable, 2 Meat, ½ Fat

Beef Stroganoff

Oven-Fried Chicken

Makes 4 servings

 4 boneless skinless chicken breasts (4 ounces each)
 4 small skinless chicken drumsticks (about 2½ ounces each)
 3 tablespoons all-purpose flour
 ½ teaspoon poultry seasoning
 ¼ teaspoon garlic salt
 ¼ teaspoon black pepper
1½ cups cornflakes, crushed
 1 tablespoon dried parsley flakes
 1 egg white
 1 tablespoon water
   Nonstick cooking spray

1. Preheat oven to 375°F. Rinse chicken. Pat dry with paper towels. Trim off any fat.

2. Combine flour, poultry seasoning, garlic salt and pepper in large resealable plastic food storage bag. Combine cornflake crumbs and parsley in shallow bowl. Whisk together egg white and water in small bowl.

3. Add chicken to flour mixture, one or two pieces at a time. Seal bag; shake until chicken is well coated. Remove chicken from bag, shaking off excess flour. Dip into egg white mixture, coating all sides. Roll in crumb mixture. Place in shallow baking pan. Repeat with remaining chicken, flour mixture, egg white mixture and crumb mixture.

4. Lightly spray chicken pieces with cooking spray. Bake breast pieces 18 to 20 minutes or until no longer pink in center. Bake drumsticks about 25 minutes or until juices run clear.

Nutrients per serving: 1 chicken breast and 1 drumstick
Calories: 314, **Calories from Fat:** 17%, **Total Fat:** 6g,
Saturated Fat: 2g, **Cholesterol:** 170mg, **Sodium:** 278mg,
Carbohydrate: 13g, **Fiber:** 1g, **Protein:** 50g

Dietary Exchange: 1 Starch, 5 Meat

Oven-Fried Chicken

Greek-Style Beef Kabobs

Makes 4 servings

 1 pound boneless beef sirloin steak (1 inch thick), cut into 16 pieces
 ¼ cup fat-free Italian salad dressing
 3 tablespoons fresh lemon juice, divided
 1 tablespoon dried oregano leaves
 1 tablespoon Worcestershire sauce
 2 teaspoons dried basil leaves
 1 teaspoon grated lemon peel
 ⅛ teaspoon dried red pepper flakes
 1 large green bell pepper, cut into 16 pieces
 16 cherry tomatoes
 2 teaspoons olive oil
 ⅛ teaspoon salt

1. Combine beef, salad dressing, 2 tablespoons lemon juice, oregano, Worcestershire sauce, basil, lemon peel and red pepper flakes in large resealable plastic food storage bag. Seal tightly; turn several times to coat. Refrigerate at least 8 hours or overnight, turning occasionally.

2. Preheat broiler. Thread 4 (10-inch) skewers with beef, alternating with pepper and tomatoes. Spray baking pan or broiler pan with nonstick cooking spray. Remove kabobs from marinade. Place on baking pan. Discard marinade. Broil kabobs 3 minutes. Turn over; broil 2 minutes or until desired doneness is reached. *Do not overcook.* Remove skewers to serving platter.

3. Add remaining 1 tablespoon lemon juice, olive oil and salt to pan drippings on baking sheet; stir well, scraping bottom of pan with flat spatula. Pour juices over kabobs.

Prep Time: 10 minutes
Marinating Time: 8 hours
Cook Time: 5 minutes

Nutrients per serving: 1 kabob (4 beef pieces, 4 pepper pieces and 4 tomatoes)
Calories: 193, **Calories from Fat:** 37%, **Total Fat:** 8g,
Saturated Fat: 2g, **Cholesterol:** 69mg, **Sodium:** 159mg,
Carbohydrate: 5g, **Fiber:** 1g, **Protein:** 25g

Dietary Exchange: 1 Vegetable, 3 Meat

Greek-Style Beef Kabob

Lemon-Dijon Chicken with Potatoes

Makes 6 servings

>   2 lemons
>   ½ cup chopped fresh parsley
>   2 tablespoons Dijon mustard
>   4 cloves garlic, minced
>   2 teaspoons extra-virgin olive oil
>   1 teaspoon dried rosemary
>   ¾ teaspoon black pepper
>   ½ teaspoon salt
>   1 whole chicken (about 3½ pounds)
>   1½ pounds small red potatoes, cut into halves

1. Preheat oven to 350°F. Squeeze 3 tablespoons juice from lemons; reserve squeezed lemon halves. Combine parsley, lemon juice, mustard, garlic, oil, rosemary, pepper and salt in small bowl; blend well. Reserve 2 tablespoons mixture.

2. Place chicken on rack in baking pan; gently slide fingers between skin and meat of chicken breasts and drumsticks to separate skin from the meat, being careful not to tear skin. Spoon remaining parsley mixture between skin and meat (secure breast skin with toothpicks, if necessary) and place lemon halves in cavity of chicken. Bake 30 minutes.

3. Meanwhile, toss potatoes with reserved parsley mixture until coated. Arrange potatoes around chicken; bake 1 hour or until juices in chicken run clear and thermometer inserted in thickest part of thigh registers 180°F. Let chicken stand 10 minutes before removing skin and slicing. Sprinkle any accumulated juices from bottom of pan over chicken and potatoes.

Nutrients per serving: ⅙ of total recipe
Calories: 294, **Calories from Fat:** 27%, **Total Fat:** 9g,
Saturated Fat: 2g, **Cholesterol:** 84mg, **Sodium:** 348mg,
Carbohydrate: 26g, **Fiber:** 3g, **Protein:** 30g

Dietary Exchange: 2 Starch, 3 Meat

Lemon-Dijon Chicken with Potatoes

Stuffed Pork Tenderloin

Makes 4 servings

⅓ cup chopped onion
2 cloves garlic, minced, divided
1 tablespoon stick butter or margarine
1 small tart apple, peeled, cored and finely chopped
¼ cup chopped pitted prunes
¼ cup dry white wine or unsweetened apple juice
2 tablespoons EQUAL® SPOONFUL*
¾ teaspoon dried rosemary leaves, divided
¾ teaspoon dried thyme leaves, divided
¼ cup cornbread stuffing crumbs
   Salt and pepper
1 whole pork tenderloin (about 16 ounces)

May substitute 3 packets EQUAL® sweetener.

• Sauté onion and 1 clove garlic in butter in medium skillet until tender, about 5 minutes. Add apple and prunes; cook 2 to 3 minutes. Add wine, Equal® and ½ teaspoon *each* rosemary and thyme; cook, covered, over medium heat about 5 minutes or until wine is evaporated. Stir in stuffing crumbs; season to taste with salt and pepper.

• Cut lengthwise slit about 2-inches deep in pork tenderloin. Mix remaining ¼ teaspoon *each* rosemary and thyme and 1 clove garlic; rub over outside surface of pork. Spoon fruit stuffing into pork and place in baking pan.

• Roast meat, uncovered, in preheated 350°F oven about 45 minutes (meat thermometer will register 160°F) or until no longer pink in center. Let stand 5 to 10 minutes before cutting into 8 slices.

Tip: The stuffing can also be used to stuff lean pork chops. Cut pockets in chops with a sharp knife, or have a butcher cut the pockets for you.

Nutrients per serving: 2 slices
Calories: 243, **Calories from Fat:** 26%, **Total Fat:** 7g,
Saturated Fat: 3g, **Cholesterol:** 74mg, **Sodium:** 117mg,
Carbohydrate: 18g, **Fiber:** 2g, **Protein:** 25g

Dietary Exchange: 1 Fruit, 3 Meat

Fruit-Stuffed Pork Tenderloin

Chicken Piccata

Makes 4 servings

- 3 tablespoons all-purpose flour
- ½ teaspoon salt
- ¼ teaspoon black pepper
- 4 boneless skinless chicken breasts (4 ounces each)
- 2 teaspoons olive oil
- 1 teaspoon butter
- 2 cloves garlic, minced
- ¾ cup canned fat-free reduced-sodium chicken broth
- 1 tablespoon fresh lemon juice
- 2 tablespoons chopped Italian parsley
- 1 tablespoon drained capers
    Lemon slices and parsley sprigs (optional)

1. Combine flour, salt and pepper in shallow pie plate. Reserve 1 tablespoon of flour mixture.

2. Place chicken between sheets of plastic wrap. Using flat side of meat mallet or rolling pin, pound chicken to ½-inch thickness. Dredge chicken in flour mixture.

3. Heat oil and butter in large nonstick skillet over medium heat until butter is melted. Cook chicken 4 to 5 minutes per side or until no longer pink in center. Transfer to serving platter; set aside.

4. Add garlic to same skillet; cook and stir over medium heat 1 minute. Add reserved flour mixture; cook and stir 1 minute. Add broth and lemon juice; cook 2 minutes, stirring frequently, until sauce thickens. Stir in parsley and capers; spoon sauce over chicken. Garnish with lemon slices and parsley sprigs, if desired.

Nutrients per serving: 1 chicken breast with about ¼ cup sauce
Calories: 194, **Calories from Fat:** 30%, **Total Fat:** 6g,
Saturated Fat: 2g, **Cholesterol:** 71mg, **Sodium:** 473mg,
Carbohydrate: 5g, **Fiber:** <1g, **Protein:** 27g

Dietary Exchange: ½ Starch, 3 Meat

Chicken Piccata

weeknight meals

Apple-Cherry Glazed Pork Chops

Makes 2 servings

- ¼ to ½ teaspoon dried thyme leaves
- ⅛ teaspoon salt
- ⅛ teaspoon black pepper
- 2 boneless pork loin chops (3 ounces each), trimmed of fat
  Nonstick olive oil cooking spray
- ⅔ cup unsweetened apple juice
- ½ small apple, cut into 6 slices
- 2 tablespoons sliced green onion
- 2 tablespoons dried tart cherries
- 1 teaspoon cornstarch
- 1 tablespoon water

1. Stir together thyme, salt and pepper. Rub on both sides of pork chops. Spray large skillet with cooking spray. Add pork chops. Cook over medium heat 3 to 5 minutes or until barely pink in center, turning once. Remove chops from skillet; keep warm.

2. Add apple juice, apple slices, green onion and cherries to same skillet. Simmer, uncovered, 2 to 3 minutes or until apple and onion are tender. Combine cornstarch and water. Stir into skillet. Bring to a boil; cook and stir until thickened. Spoon over pork chops.

Nutrients per serving: 1 pork chop with 3 apple slices and about ½ cup apple-cherry glaze
Calories: 243, **Calories from Fat:** 31%, **Total Fat:** 8g,
Saturated Fat: 3g, **Cholesterol:** 40mg, **Sodium:** 191mg,
Carbohydrate: 23g, **Fiber:** 1g, **Protein:** 19g

Dietary Exchange: 1½ Fruit, 2 Meat, 1 Fat

Apple-Cherry Glazed Pork Chop

Gingered Chicken with Vegetables

Makes 4 servings

- 2 tablespoons vegetable oil, divided
- 1 pound boneless skinless chicken breasts, cut into thin strips
- 1 cup red bell pepper strips
- 1 cup sliced fresh mushrooms
- 16 fresh pea pods, cut in half crosswise
- ½ cup sliced water chestnuts
- ¼ cup sliced green onions
- 1 tablespoon grated fresh gingerroot
- 1 large clove garlic, crushed
- ⅔ cup reduced-fat, reduced-sodium chicken broth
- 2 tablespoons **EQUAL® SPOONFUL***
- 2 tablespoons light soy sauce
- 4 teaspoons cornstarch
- 2 teaspoons dark sesame oil
  Salt and pepper to taste

May substitute 3 packets EQUAL® sweetener.

• Heat 1 tablespoon vegetable oil in large skillet over medium-high heat. Stir-fry chicken until no longer pink; remove chicken from skillet. Heat remaining 1 tablespoon vegetable oil in skillet. Add bell peppers, mushrooms, pea pods, water chestnuts, green onions, ginger and garlic to skillet. Stir-fry mixture 3 to 4 minutes until vegetables are crisp-tender.

• Meanwhile, combine chicken broth, Equal®, soy sauce, cornstarch and sesame oil until smooth. Stir into skillet mixture. Cook over medium heat until thick and clear. Stir in chicken; heat through. Season with salt and pepper to taste.

• Serve over hot cooked rice, if desired.

Nutrients per serving: ¼ of total recipe
Calories: 263, **Calories from Fat:** 38%, **Total Fat:** 11g,
Saturated Fat: 1g, **Cholesterol:** 66mg, **Sodium:** 411mg,
Carbohydrate: 11g, **Fiber:** 2g, **Protein:** 29g

Dietary Exchange: 2 Vegetable, 4 Meat

Gingered Chicken with Vegetables

Buttery Pepper and Citrus Broiled Fish

Makes 4 servings

- 3 tablespoons MOLLY MCBUTTER® Flavored Sprinkles
- 1 tablespoon MRS. DASH® Lemon Pepper Blend
- 1 tablespoon lime juice
- 2 teaspoons honey
- 1 pound (1-inch thick) boneless white fish fillets (4 ounces each)

Combine first 4 ingredients in small bowl; mix well. Broil fish 6 to 8 inches from heat about 6 minutes; turning once. Spread with Lemon Pepper mixture. Broil an additional 4 to 5 minutes.

Preparation Time: 5 minutes
Cooking Time: 10 minutes

Nutrients per serving: 1 fillet
Calories: 117, **Calories from Fat:** 8%, **Total Fat:** 1g,
Saturated Fat: <1g, **Cholesterol:** 49mg, **Sodium:** 424mg,
Carbohydrate: 6g, **Fiber:** 1g, **Protein:** 20g

Dietary Exchange: 1 Starch, 2 Meat

Buttery Pepper and Citrus Broiled Fish

Basil Pork and Green Bean Stew

Makes 6 servings

  1   package (9 ounces) frozen cut green beans
3½ cups peeled red potatoes cut into ½-inch cubes
  1   pound trimmed pork tenderloin, cut into 1-inch cubes
  1   cup no-sugar-added pasta sauce
 ½ teaspoon salt
  1   tablespoon chopped fresh basil *or* 1 teaspoon dried basil leaves
 ¼ cup grated Parmesan cheese

MICROWAVE DIRECTIONS

1. Place beans in 10- to 12-inch microwavable casserole. Microwave, covered, at HIGH 2 minutes. Drain in colander.

2. Using same dish, microwave potatoes, covered, at HIGH 3 minutes. Stir in pork, beans, pasta sauce and salt. Microwave at HIGH 10 minutes, stirring halfway through. Stir in basil. Microwave 5 to 7 minutes or until potatoes are tender and meat is no longer pink in center. Sprinkle with cheese.

Nutrients per serving: ⅙ of total recipe
Calories: 274, **Calories from Fat:** 13%, **Total Fat:** 4g,
Saturated Fat: 2g, **Cholesterol:** 46mg, **Sodium:** 504mg,
Carbohydrate: 39g, **Fiber:** 6g, **Protein:** 21g

Dietary Exchange: 2 Starch, 1 Vegetable, 2 Meat

Basil Pork and Green Bean Stew

Broccoli, Chicken and Rice Casserole

Makes 4 servings

> 1 box UNCLE BEN'S CHEF'S RECIPE® Broccoli Rice Au Gratin Supreme
> 2 cups boiling water
> 4 boneless, skinless chicken breasts (about 1 pound)
> ¼ teaspoon garlic powder
> 2 cups frozen broccoli
> 1 cup (4 ounces) reduced-fat shredded Cheddar cheese

1. Heat oven to 425°F. In 13×9-inch baking pan, combine rice and contents of seasoning packet. Add boiling water; mix well. Add chicken; sprinkle with garlic powder. Cover and bake 30 minutes.

2. Add broccoli and cheese; continue to bake, covered, 8 to 10 minutes or until chicken is no longer pink in center.

Nutrients per serving: ¼ of total recipe
Calories: 353, **Calories from Fat:** 24%, **Total Fat:** 10g,
Saturated Fat: 5g, **Cholesterol:** 87mg, **Sodium:** 778mg,
Carbohydrate: 31g, **Fiber:** 3g, **Protein:** 37g

Dietary Exchange: 1½ Starch, 1 Vegetable, 4 Meat

Broccoli, Chicken and Rice Casserole

Saucy Tomato-Pork Skillet

Makes 4 servings

> 1 cup uncooked instant white rice
> ⅔ cup reduced-sodium tomato juice
> 2 tablespoons reduced-sodium soy sauce
> 1 tablespoon cornstarch
> ¼ teaspoon paprika
> 3 boneless pork chops, ¾ inch thick (about ¾ pound)
> ¼ teaspoon garlic salt
> ⅛ teaspoon red pepper flakes
> 2 slices uncooked bacon, chopped
> 3 medium tomatoes, chopped
> 2 green onions with tops, sliced diagonally

1. Prepare rice according to package directions; set aside.

2. Combine tomato juice, soy sauce, cornstarch and paprika in small bowl, stirring until cornstarch dissolves. Set aside.

3. Slice pork across grain into ¼-inch slices; place in medium bowl. Sprinkle pork with garlic salt and pepper flakes; mix well.

4. Cook bacon in medium skillet over medium-high heat. Remove bacon from skillet using slotted spoon; set aside. Add pork, tomatoes and green onions to skillet; stir-fry over medium-high heat 3 minutes or until pork is barely pink in center. Stir in tomato juice mixture; cook, stirring constantly, 1 minute or until sauce thickens slightly. Remove from heat; stir in bacon.

5. Serve pork mixture over rice.

Prep and Cook Time: 28 minutes

Nutrients per serving: 1½ cups pork mixture with ½ cup cooked rice
Calories: 307, **Calories from Fat:** 32%, **Total Fat:** 10g,
Saturated Fat: 3g, **Cholesterol:** 62mg, **Sodium:** 492mg,
Carbohydrate: 26g, **Fiber:** 1g, **Protein:** 23g

Dietary Exchange: 1½ Starch, 1 Vegetable, 2 Meat, 1 Fat

Saucy Tomato-Pork Skillet

Cheesy Tuna Mac

Makes 4 servings

- 8 **ounces uncooked elbow macaroni**
- 2 **tablespoons margarine or butter**
- 2 **tablespoons all-purpose flour**
- 1 **teaspoon paprika**
- ¼ **teaspoon salt**
- 1 **cup canned reduced-sodium chicken broth**
- 6 **ounces reduced-fat reduced-sodium cheese spread, cut into cubes**
- 1 **can (6 ounces) tuna packed in water, drained and flaked**

1. Cook macaroni according to package directions, omitting salt. Drain; set aside.

2. Melt margarine in medium saucepan over medium heat. Add flour, paprika and salt; cook and stir 1 minute. Add broth; bring to a simmer for 2 minutes or until sauce thickens.

3. Add cheese spread; cook and stir until cheese melts. Combine tuna and pasta in medium bowl; pour sauce mixture over tuna mixture; toss to coat. Sprinkle with additional paprika, if desired.

Nutrients per serving: ¼ of total recipe
Calories: 284, **Calories from Fat:** 32%, **Total Fat:** 10g,
Saturated Fat: 3g, **Cholesterol:** 34mg, **Sodium:** 448mg,
Carbohydrate: 21g, **Fiber:** 1g, **Protein:** 27g

Dietary Exchange: 1½ Starch, 3 Meat

Cheesy Tuna Mac

Chicken with Spinach and Celery Hash

Makes 4 servings

- 1 **package (16-ounces) refrigerated, precooked, fat-free hash browns**
- 1 **package (8 ounces) ready-to-use celery sticks, thinly sliced**
- 3 **teaspoons olive oil, divided**
- 12 **chicken tenders (about 1 pound)**
- ½ **teaspoon dried thyme leaves**
- ¼ **teaspoon ground white pepper**
- 2 **packages (5 ounces each) ready-to-use baby spinach**
- ¼ **cup water**

1. Combine hash-browns and celery in medium bowl.

2. Heat 1½ teaspoons oil in large nonstick skillet over medium-high heat. Add potato mixture and cook about 10 minutes, stirring and turning occasionally, or until hash brown mixture begins to brown. Reduce heat; cook 10 minutes until hash brown mixture is browned.

3. Meanwhile, heat remaining 1½ teaspoons oil in 12-inch nonstick skillet over medium-high heat until hot. Add chicken tenders. Sprinkle tenders with thyme and pepper. Cook about 5 minutes, turning once, or until no longer pink. Remove and keep warm.

4. To same skillet, add spinach and water. Cover; cook about 3 minutes, stirring once.

5. To serve, divide spinach and hash into four portions and top with 3 chicken tenders per plate.

Nutrients per serving: ¼ of total recipe
Calories: 294, **Calories from Fat:** 27%, **Total Fat:** 9g,
Saturated Fat: 1g, **Cholesterol:** 65mg, **Sodium:** 217mg,
Carbohydrate: 22g, **Fiber:** 8g, **Protein:** 31g

Dietary Exchange: 1 Starch, 1 Vegetable, 3 Meat

Chicken with Spinach and Celery Hash

Mediterranean Sandwiches

Makes 6 servings

 Nonstick cooking spray
1¼ pounds chicken tenders, cut crosswise in half
 1 large tomato, cut into bite-size pieces
 ½ small cucumber, seeded and sliced
 ½ cup sweet onion slices (about 1 small)
 2 tablespoons cider vinegar
 1 tablespoon olive oil or canola oil
 3 teaspoons minced fresh oregano *or* ½ teaspoon dried oregano leaves
 2 teaspoons minced fresh mint *or* ¼ teaspoon dried mint leaves
 ¼ teaspoon salt
 6 rounds whole wheat pita bread
12 lettuce leaves (optional)

1. Spray large nonstick skillet with cooking spray; heat over medium heat until hot. Add chicken; cook and stir 7 to 10 minutes or until browned and no longer pink in center. Cool slightly.

2. Combine chicken, tomato, cucumber and onion in medium bowl. Drizzle with vinegar and oil; toss to coat. Sprinkle with oregano, mint and salt; toss to combine.

3. Cut pitas in half crosswise; gently open. Place 1 lettuce leaf in each pita bread half, if desired. Divide chicken mixture evenly among pita bread halves.

Nutrients per serving: 2 filled pita halves
Calories: 242, **Calories from Fat:** 21%, **Total Fat:** 6g,
Saturated Fat: 1g, **Cholesterol:** 50mg, **Sodium:** 353mg,
Carbohydrate: 24g, **Fiber:** 2g, **Protein:** 23g

Dietary Exchange: 1½ Starch, 2½ Meat

Mediterranean Sandwiches

soups & salads

Chicken and Spinach Salad

Makes 4 servings

- 12 ounces chicken tenders
  Nonstick cooking spray
- 4 cups washed, stemmed and shredded spinach
- 2 cups washed and torn romaine lettuce
- 8 thin slices red onion, separated into rings
- 2 tablespoons (½ ounce) crumbled blue cheese
- 1 large grapefruit, peeled and sectioned
- ½ cup frozen citrus blend concentrate, thawed
- ¼ cup prepared fat-free Italian salad dressing

1. Cut chicken into 2×½-inch strips. Spray large nonstick skillet with cooking spray; heat over medium heat until hot. Add chicken; cook and stir 5 minutes or until no longer pink in center. Remove from skillet; set aside.

2. Divide spinach, lettuce, onion, cheese, grapefruit and chicken among 4 salad plates. Combine citrus blend concentrate and Italian dressing in small bowl; drizzle over salads. Garnish with assorted greens, if desired.

Nutrients per serving: ¼ of total recipe
Calories: 218, **Calories from Fat:** 15%, **Total Fat:** 4g,
Saturated Fat: 1g, **Cholesterol:** 55mg, **Sodium:** 361mg,
Carbohydrate: 23g, **Fiber:** 3g, **Protein:** 23g

Dietary Exchange: 1 Fruit, 2 Vegetable, 2 Meat

Chicken and Spinach Salad

Chunky Chicken and Vegetable Soup

Makes 4 servings

- 1 tablespoon canola oil
- 1 boneless skinless chicken breast (4 ounces), diced
- ½ cup chopped green bell pepper
- ½ cup thinly sliced celery
- 2 green onions, sliced
- 2 cans (14½ ounces each) chicken broth
- 1 cup water
- ½ cup sliced carrots
- 2 tablespoons cream
- 1 tablespoon finely chopped fresh parsley
- ¼ teaspoon dried thyme leaves
- ⅛ teaspoon black pepper

1. Heat oil in large saucepan over medium heat. Add chicken; cook and stir 4 to 5 minutes or until no longer pink. Add bell pepper, celery and onions. Cook and stir 7 minutes or until vegetables are tender.

2. Add broth, water, carrots, cream, parsley, thyme and black pepper. Simmer 10 minutes or until carrots are tender.

Nutrients per serving: ¼ of total recipe
Calories: 130, **Calories from Fat:** 57%, **Total Fat:** 8g,
Saturated Fat: 3g, **Cholesterol:** 27mg, **Sodium:** 895mg,
Carbohydrate: 5g, **Fiber:** 1g, **Protein:** 9g

Dietary Exchange: 1 Vegetable, 1 Meat, 1 Fat

Chunky Chicken and Vegetable Soup

Turkey, Mandarin and Poppy Seed Salad

Makes 4 servings

¼ cup orange juice
1½ tablespoons red wine vinegar
1½ teaspoons poppy seeds
1½ teaspoons olive oil
1 teaspoon Dijon-style mustard
⅛ teaspoon ground pepper
5 cups torn stemmed washed red leaf lettuce
2 cups torn stemmed washed spinach
½ pound honey roasted turkey breast, cut into ½-inch julienne strips
1 can (10½ ounces) mandarin oranges, drained

In small bowl, combine orange juice, vinegar, poppy seeds, oil, mustard and pepper. Set aside. In large bowl, toss together lettuce, spinach, turkey and oranges. Pour dressing over turkey mixture and serve immediately.

*Favorite recipe from **National Turkey Federation***

Nutrients per serving: ¼ of total recipe
Calories: 136, **Calories from Fat:** 23%, **Total Fat:** 4g,
Saturated Fat: <1g, **Cholesterol:** 20mg, **Sodium:** 688mg,
Carbohydrate: 15g, **Fiber:** 2g, **Protein:** 13g

Dietary Exchange: ½ Fruit, 1 Vegetable, 2 Meat

Turkey, Mandarin and Poppy Seed Salad

Kansas City Steak Soup

Makes 6 servings

    Nonstick cooking spray
½   pound 95% lean ground beef
1   cup chopped onion
3   cups frozen mixed vegetables
2   cups water
1   can (14½ ounces) stewed tomatoes, undrained
1   cup sliced celery
1   beef bouillon cube
½ to 1 teaspoon black pepper
1   can (10½ ounces) fat-free beef broth
½   cup all-purpose flour

1. Spray Dutch oven with cooking spray. Heat over medium-high heat until hot. Add beef and onion. Cook and stir 5 minutes or until beef is browned.

2. Add vegetables, water, tomatoes with juice, celery, bouillon cube and pepper. Bring to a boil. Whisk together beef broth and flour until smooth; add to beef mixture, stirring constantly. Return mixture to a boil. Reduce heat to low. Cover and simmer 15 minutes, stirring frequently.

Note: If time permits, allow the soup to simmer an additional 30 minutes. The flavors just get better and better!

Nutrients per serving: 1⅔ cups soup
Calories: 198, **Calories from Fat:** 23%, **Total Fat:** 5g,
Saturated Fat: 2g, **Cholesterol:** 23mg, **Sodium:** 598mg,
Carbohydrate: 27g, **Fiber:** 5g, **Protein:** 13g

Dietary Exchange: ½ Starch, 3½ Vegetable, 1 Meat, ½ Fat

Kansas City Steak Soup

Tangy Apple Slaw

Makes 6 servings

4	cups shredded green cabbage
1	cup shredded carrots
1	cup chopped unpeeled apple (1 medium)
½	cup thinly sliced red or green bell pepper strips
⅔	cup light mayonnaise or salad dressing
⅓	cup reduced-fat sour cream
3	tablespoons EQUAL® SPOONFUL*
1½	tablespoons Dijon mustard
1	tablespoon lemon juice
⅛	teaspoon pepper

May substitute 4½ packets EQUAL® sweetener.

• Combine cabbage, carrots, apple and bell pepper in medium bowl. Mix mayonnaise, sour cream, Equal®, mustard, lemon juice and pepper in small bowl; stir until well blended. Spoon Equal® mixture over cabbage mixture; gently toss to combine. Refrigerate, covered, 1 to 2 hours to allow flavors to blend.

Nutrients per serving:
Calories: 152, **Total Fat:** 11g, **Cholesterol:** 15mg, **Sodium:** 331mg, **Carbohydrate:** 13g, **Protein:** 2g

Dietary Exchange: 2 Vegetable, 2 Fat

Tangy Apple Slaw

Vegetable Beef Noodle Soup

Makes 6 servings

> 8 ounces cubed beef for stew (½-inch pieces)
> ¾ cup cubed unpeeled potato (1 medium)
> ½ cup carrot slices
> 1 tablespoon balsamic vinegar
> ¾ teaspoon dried thyme leaves
> ¼ teaspoon black pepper
> 2½ cups fat-free reduced-sodium beef broth
> 1 cup water
> ¼ cup prepared chili sauce or ketchup
> 2 ounces uncooked thin egg noodles
> ¾ cup bottled or canned pearl onions, rinsed and drained
> ¼ cup frozen peas

1. Heat large saucepan over high heat until hot; add beef. Cook 3 minutes or until browned on all sides, stirring occasionally. Remove from pan.

2. Cook potato, carrot, vinegar, thyme and pepper 3 minutes in same saucepan over medium heat. Add beef broth, water and chili sauce. Bring to a boil over medium-high heat; add beef. Reduce heat to medium-low; simmer, covered, 30 minutes or until meat is almost fork-tender.

3. Bring beef mixture to a boil over medium-high heat. Add pasta; cook, covered, 7 to 10 minutes or until pasta is tender, stirring occasionally. Add onions and peas; heat 1 minute. Serve immediately.

Nutrients per serving: 1½ cups soup
Calories: 182, **Calories from Fat:** 14%, **Total Fat:** 3g,
Saturated Fat: 1g, **Cholesterol:** 28mg, **Sodium:** 258mg,
Carbohydrate: 24g, **Fiber:** 1g, **Protein:** 15g

Dietary Exchange: 1 Starch, 1 Vegetable, 1½ Meat

Vegetable Beef Noodle Soup

Pasta and Tuna Filled Peppers

Makes 4 servings

- ¾ **cup uncooked ditalini pasta**
- 4 **large green bell peppers**
- 1 **cup chopped seeded tomatoes**
- 1 **can (6 ounces) white tuna packed in water, drained and flaked**
- ½ **cup chopped celery**
- ½ **cup (2 ounces) shredded reduced-fat Cheddar cheese**
- ¼ **cup fat-free mayonnaise or salad dressing**
- 1 **teaspoon salt-free garlic and herb seasoning**
- 2 **tablespoons shredded reduced-fat Cheddar cheese (optional)**

1. Cook pasta according to package directions, omitting salt. Rinse and drain. Set aside.

2. Cut thin slice from top of each pepper. Remove seeds and membranes from insides of peppers. Rinse peppers; place, cut side down, on paper towels to drain.*

3. Combine cooked pasta, tomatoes, tuna, celery, ½ cup cheese, mayonnaise and seasoning in large bowl until well blended; spoon evenly into pepper shells.

4. Place peppers on large microwavable plate; cover with waxed paper. Microwave at HIGH (100% power) 7 to 8 minutes, turning halfway through cooking time. Top evenly with remaining 2 tablespoons cheese before serving, if desired. Garnish as desired.

For more tender peppers, cook in boiling water 2 minutes. Rinse with cold water; drain upside down on paper towels before filling.

Nutrients per serving: 1 filled pepper (without cheese topping and garnish)
Calories: 216, **Calories from Fat:** 16%, **Total Fat:** 4g,
Saturated Fat: 1g, **Cholesterol:** 26mg, **Sodium:** 574mg,
Carbohydrate: 27g, **Fiber:** 2g, **Protein:** 19g

Dietary Exchange: 1½ Starch, 1 Vegetable, 2 Meat

Pasta and Tuna Filled Pepper

Double Corn & Cheddar Chowder

Makes 6 servings

1	tablespoon margarine
1	cup chopped onion
2	tablespoons all-purpose flour
2½	cups fat-free reduced-sodium chicken broth
1	can (16 ounces) cream-style corn
1	cup frozen whole kernel corn
½	cup finely diced red bell pepper
½	teaspoon hot pepper sauce
¾	cup (3 ounces) shredded sharp Cheddar cheese
	Black pepper (optional)

1. Melt margarine in large saucepan over medium heat. Add onion; cook and stir 5 minutes. Sprinkle onion with flour; cook and stir 1 minute.

2. Add chicken broth; bring to a boil, stirring frequently. Add cream-style corn, corn kernels, bell pepper and pepper sauce; bring to a simmer. Cover; simmer 15 minutes.

3. Remove from heat; gradually stir in cheese until melted. Ladle into soup bowls; sprinkle with black pepper, if desired.

Nutrients per serving: ⅙ of total recipe
Calories: 180, **Calories from Fat:** 28%, **Total Fat:** 6g,
Saturated Fat: 2g, **Cholesterol:** 10mg, **Sodium:** 498mg,
Carbohydrate: 28g, **Fiber:** 2g, **Protein:** 7g

Dietary Exchange: 1½ Starch, ½ Meat, 1 Fat

Double Corn & Cheddar Chowder

Ginger Shrimp Salad

Makes 3 servings

1 package (10 ounces) DOLE® French Salad Blend or Italian Salad Blend

6 ounces cooked shelled and deveined medium shrimp or cooked tiny shrimp

1 can (11 or 15 ounces) DOLE® Mandarin Oranges, drained

1 medium DOLE® Red, Yellow or Green Bell Pepper, cut into 2-inch strips

⅓ cup fat free or reduced fat mayonnaise

⅓ cup DOLE® Pineapple Juice

2 teaspoons finely chopped fresh ginger *or* ¼ teaspoon ground ginger

• Toss salad blend, shrimp, mandarin oranges and bell pepper in large serving bowl.

• Stir mayonnaise, juice and ginger in small bowl. Add to salad; toss to evenly coat.

Prep Time: 20 minutes

Nutrients per serving: about 3½ cups salad
Calories: 156, **Calories from Fat:** 4%, **Total Fat:** 1g,
Saturated Fat: <1g, **Cholesterol:** 111mg, **Sodium:** 358mg,
Carbohydrate: 22g, **Fiber:** 3g, **Protein:** 14g

Dietary Exchange: 1 Fruit, 1 Vegetable, 2 Meat

Ginger Shrimp Salad

favorite
desserts

Baked Pear Dessert

Makes 2 servings

> 2 tablespoons dried cranberries or raisins
> 1 tablespoon toasted sliced almonds
> ⅓ cup unsweetened apple cider or apple juice, divided
> ⅛ teaspoon ground cinnamon
> 1 medium (6-ounce) unpeeled pear, cut in half lengthwise and cored
> ½ cup vanilla low-fat no-sugar-added frozen ice cream or frozen yogurt

1. Preheat oven to 350°F. Combine cranberries, almonds, 1 teaspoon cider and cinnamon in small bowl.

2. Place pear halves, cut sides up, in small baking dish. Evenly mound almond mixture on top of pear halves. Pour remaining cider into dish. Cover with foil.

3. Bake pear halves 35 to 40 minutes or until pears are soft, spooning cider in dish over pears once or twice during baking. Serve warm with ice cream.

Nutrients per serving: 1 topped pear half with ¼ cup ice cream
Calories: 87, **Calories from Fat:** 19%, **Total Fat:** 2g,
Saturated Fat: <1g, **Cholesterol:** 3mg, **Sodium:** 13mg,
Carbohydrate: 16g, **Fiber:** 1g, **Protein:** 1g

Dietary Exchange: 1 Fruit, ½ Fat

Baked Pear Dessert

Lemon Poppy Seed Bundt Cake

Makes 16 servings

> 1 **cup granulated sugar**
> ½ **cup (1 stick) butter, softened**
> 1 **egg, at room temperature**
> 2 **egg whites, at room temperature**
> ¾ **cup low-fat (1%) milk**
> 2 **teaspoons vanilla**
> 2 **cups all-purpose flour**
> 2 **tablespoons poppy seeds**
> 1 **tablespoon grated lemon peel**
> 2 **teaspoons baking powder**
> ¼ **teaspoon salt**
> 4½ **teaspoons powdered sugar**

1. Preheat oven to 350°F. Grease and flour Bundt pan; set aside.

2. Beat granulated sugar, butter, egg and egg whites in large bowl with electric mixer at medium speed until well blended. Add milk and vanilla; mix well. Add flour, poppy seeds, lemon peel, baking powder and salt; beat about 2 minutes or until smooth.

3. Pour into prepared pan. Bake 30 minutes or until toothpick inserted near center comes out clean. Gently loosen cake from pan with knife; turn out onto wire rack. Cool completely. Sprinkle with powdered sugar. Garnish as desired. Cut into 16 pieces before serving.

Nutrients per serving: 1 piece cake
Calories: 178, **Calories from Fat:** 35%, **Total Fat:** 7g,
Saturated Fat: 1g, **Cholesterol:** 14mg, **Sodium:** 181mg,
Carbohydrate: 26g, **Fiber:** 1g, **Protein:** 3g

Dietary Exchange: 1½ Starch, 1½ Fat

Lemon Poppy Seed Bundt Cake

Rich Chocolate Cheesecake

Makes 16 servings

- 1 cup chocolate wafer crumbs
- 3 tablespoons **EQUAL® SPOONFUL***
- 3 tablespoons stick butter or margarine, melted
- 3 packages (8 ounces each) reduced-fat cream cheese, softened
- 1¼ cups **EQUAL® SPOONFUL****
- 2 eggs
- 2 egg whites
- 2 tablespoons cornstarch
- ¼ teaspoon salt
- 1 cup reduced-fat sour cream
- 2 teaspoons vanilla
- 4 ounces (4 squares) semi-sweet chocolate, melted and slightly cooled

*May substitute 4½ packets EQUAL® sweetener.

**May substitute 30 packets EQUAL® sweetener.

• Mix chocolate crumbs, 3 tablespoons Equal® Spoonful and melted butter in bottom of 9-inch springform pan. Pat mixture evenly onto bottom of pan. Bake in preheated 325°F oven 8 minutes. Cool on wire rack.

• Beat cream cheese and 1¼ cups Equal® Spoonful in large bowl until fluffy; beat in eggs, egg whites, cornstarch and salt. Beat in sour cream and vanilla until well blended. Gently fold in melted chocolate. Pour batter into crust.

• Bake in 325°F oven 40 to 45 minutes or until center is almost set. Remove cheesecake to wire rack. Gently run metal spatula around rim of pan to loosen cake. Let cheesecake cool completely; cover and refrigerate several hours or overnight before serving. To serve, remove side of springform pan.

Nutrients per serving: ¹⁄₁₆ of total recipe
Calories: 219, **Calories from Fat:** 58%, **Total Fat:** 14g,
Saturated Fat: 9g, **Cholesterol:** 57mg, **Sodium:** 313mg,
Carbohydrate: 15g, **Fiber:** 1g, **Protein:** 7g

Dietary Exchange: 1 Starch, 3 Fat

Rich Chocolate Cheesecake

Hidden Pumpkin Pies

Makes 6 servings

1½ **cups solid-pack pumpkin**
1 **cup evaporated skimmed milk**
½ **cup cholesterol-free egg substitute *or* 2 eggs**
¼ **cup sugar substitute (sucralose-based)**
1 **teaspoon pumpkin pie spice***
1¼ **teaspoons vanilla, divided**
3 **egg whites**
¼ **teaspoon cream of tartar**
⅓ **cup honey**

*Substitute ½ teaspoon ground cinnamon, ¼ teaspoon ground ginger and ⅛ teaspoon each ground allspice and ground nutmeg for 1 teaspoon pumpkin pie spice.

1. Preheat oven to 350°F.

2. Stir together pumpkin, evaporated milk, egg substitute, sugar substitute, pumpkin pie spice and 1 teaspoon vanilla. Pour into 6 (6-ounce) custard cups or 6 (¾-cup) soufflé dishes. Place in shallow baking dish or pan. Pour boiling water around custard cups to depth of 1 inch. Bake 25 minutes.

3. Meanwhile, beat egg whites, cream of tartar and remaining ¼ teaspoon vanilla at high speed of electric mixer until soft peaks form. Gradually add honey, beating until stiff peaks form.

4. Spread egg white mixture on tops of hot pumpkin mixture. Return to oven. Bake 15 to 16 minutes or until tops are golden brown. Let stand 10 minutes. Serve warm.

Nutrients per serving: 1 pie
Calories: 148, **Calories from Fat:** 10%, **Total Fat:** 2g, **Saturated Fat:** 1g, **Cholesterol:** 54mg, **Sodium:** 133mg, **Carbohydrate:** 27g, **Fiber:** 2g, **Protein:** 8g

Dietary Exchange: 2 Starch, 1 Meat

Hidden Pumpkin Pie

Cranberry Apple Crisp

Makes 8 servings

3 cups peeled and sliced apples
2 cups fresh cranberries
1 cup EQUAL® SPOONFUL*
½ cup EQUAL® SPOONFUL**
⅓ cup all-purpose flour
¼ cup chopped pecans
¼ cup stick butter or margarine, melted

May substitute 24 packets EQUAL® sweetener.

**May substitute 12 packets EQUAL® sweetener.*

• Combine apples, cranberries and 1 cup Equal® Spoonful in ungreased 10-inch pie pan.

• Combine ½ cup Equal® Spoonful, flour, pecans and butter in separate bowl. Sprinkle mixture over top of apples and cranberries.

• Bake in preheated 350°F oven about 1 hour or until bubbly and lightly browned.

Tip: This crisp is delicious served as an accompaniment to pork or poultry or with frozen yogurt as a dessert.

Nutrients per serving: ½ cup crisp (without frozen yogurt)
Calories: 150, **Calories from Fat:** 50%, **Total Fat:** 9g,
Saturated Fat: 4g, **Cholesterol:** 16mg, **Sodium:** 62mg,
Carbohydrate: 18g, **Fiber:** 3g, **Protein:** 1g

Dietary Exchange: 1 Fruit, 2 Fat

Cranberry Apple Crisp

Peaches & Cream Gingersnap Cups

Makes 2 servings

- 1½ tablespoons gingersnap crumbs (2 cookies)
- ¼ teaspoon ground ginger
- 2 ounces reduced-fat cream cheese, softened
- 1 container (6 ounces) peach sugar-free nonfat yogurt
- ¼ teaspoon vanilla
- ⅓ cup chopped fresh peach or drained canned peach slices in juice

1. Combine gingersnap crumbs and ginger in small bowl; set aside.

2. Beat cream cheese in small bowl at medium speed of electric mixer until smooth. Add yogurt and vanilla. Beat at low speed until smooth and well blended. Stir in chopped peach.

3. Divide peach mixture between two 6-ounce custard cups. Cover and refrigerate 1 hour. Top each serving with half of gingersnap crumb mixture just before serving. Garnish as desired.

Note: Instead of crushing the gingersnaps, serve them whole with the peaches & cream cups.

Nutrients per serving: 1 dessert cup (½ of total recipe)
Calories: 148, **Calories from Fat:** 34%, **Total Fat:** 5g,
Saturated Fat: 3g, **Cholesterol:** 16mg, **Sodium:** 204mg,
Carbohydrate: 18g, **Fiber:** 1g, **Protein:** 6g

Dietary Exchange: 1 Starch, ½ Milk, 1 Fat

Peaches & Cream Gingersnap Cups

Creamy Strawberry-Banana Tart

Makes 10 servings

- 1 package (16 ounces) frozen unsweetened whole strawberries, thawed
- 2 tablespoons plus 1½ teaspoons frozen orange juice concentrate, thawed and divided
- ¼ cup sugar
- 1 envelope unflavored gelatin
- 3 egg whites, beaten
- 1 package (3 ounces) soft ladyfingers, split
- 4 teaspoons water
- ½ container (8 ounces) frozen reduced-fat nondairy whipped topping, thawed
- 1 medium banana, quartered lengthwise and sliced
- 1 teaspoon multi-colored decorator sprinkles (optional)

1. Place thawed strawberries and 2 tablespoons orange juice concentrate in blender container or food processor bowl. Blend or process until smooth.

2. Stir together sugar and gelatin in medium saucepan. Stir in strawberry mixture. Cook, stirring frequently, until mixture comes to a boil.

3. Stir about half of mixture into beaten egg whites; return mixture to saucepan. Cook, stirring constantly, over medium heat about 2 minutes or until slightly thickened. *Do not boil.*

4. Pour into bowl. Refrigerate 2 to 2½ hours or until mixture mounds when spooned, stirring occasionally.

5. Cut half of ladyfingers in half horizontally. Place around edge of 9-inch tart pan with removable bottom. Place remaining ladyfingers into bottom of pan, cutting to fit.

6. Stir together remaining 1½ teaspoons orange juice concentrate and water. Drizzle over ladyfingers.

7. Fold thawed dessert topping and banana into strawberry mixture. Spoon into ladyfinger crust. Refrigerate at least 2 hours. Sprinkle with multi-colored sprinkles, if desired. Cut into 10 wedges to serve.

Nutrients per serving: 1 tart wedge
Calories: 113, **Calories from Fat:** 19%, **Total Fat:** 2g,
Saturated Fat: 2g, **Cholesterol:** 31mg, **Sodium:** 32mg,
Carbohydrate: 20g, **Fiber:** 1g, **Protein:** 3g

Dietary Exchange: ½ Starch, 1 Fruit, ½ Fat

Creamy Strawberry-Banana Tart

acknowledgments

The publisher would like to thank the companies and organizations listed below for the use of their recipes and photographs in this publication.

Dole Food Company, Inc.

Egg Beaters®

Equal® sweetener

MASTERFOODS USA

Mrs. Dash®

National Turkey Federation

SPLENDA® is a trademark of McNeil Nutritionals, LLC

index

METRIC CONVERSION CHART

VOLUME MEASUREMENTS (dry)

$\frac{1}{8}$ teaspoon = 0.5 mL
$\frac{1}{4}$ teaspoon = 1 mL
$\frac{1}{2}$ teaspoon = 2 mL
$\frac{3}{4}$ teaspoon = 4 mL
1 teaspoon = 5 mL
1 tablespoon = 15 mL
2 tablespoons = 30 mL
$\frac{1}{4}$ cup = 60 mL
$\frac{1}{3}$ cup = 75 mL
$\frac{1}{2}$ cup = 125 mL
$\frac{2}{3}$ cup = 150 mL
$\frac{3}{4}$ cup = 175 mL
1 cup = 250 mL
2 cups = 1 pint = 500 mL
3 cups = 750 mL
4 cups = 1 quart = 1 L

VOLUME MEASUREMENTS (fluid)

1 fluid ounce (2 tablespoons) = 30 mL
4 fluid ounces ($\frac{1}{2}$ cup) = 125 mL
8 fluid ounces (1 cup) = 250 mL
12 fluid ounces ($1\frac{1}{2}$ cups) = 375 mL
16 fluid ounces (2 cups) = 500 mL

WEIGHTS (mass)

$\frac{1}{2}$ ounce = 15 g
1 ounce = 30 g
3 ounces = 90 g
4 ounces = 120 g
8 ounces = 225 g
10 ounces = 285 g
12 ounces = 360 g
16 ounces = 1 pound = 450 g

DIMENSIONS

$\frac{1}{16}$ inch = 2 mm
$\frac{1}{8}$ inch = 3 mm
$\frac{1}{4}$ inch = 6 mm
$\frac{1}{2}$ inch = 1.5 cm
$\frac{3}{4}$ inch = 2 cm
1 inch = 2.5 cm

OVEN TEMPERATURES

250°F = 120°C
275°F = 140°C
300°F = 150°C
325°F = 160°C
350°F = 180°C
375°F = 190°C
400°F = 200°C
425°F = 220°C
450°F = 230°C

BAKING PAN SIZES

Utensil	Size in Inches/Quarts	Metric Volume	Size in Centimeters
Baking or	8×8×2	2 L	20×20×5
Cake Pan	9×9×2	2.5 L	23×23×5
(square or	12×8×2	3 L	30×20×5
rectangular)	13×9×2	3.5 L	33×23×5
Loaf Pan	8×4×3	1.5 L	20×10×7
	9×5×3	2 L	23×13×7
Round Layer	8×1½	1.2 L	20×4
Cake Pan	9×1½	1.5 L	23×4
Pie Plate	8×1¼	750 mL	20×3
	9×1¼	1 L	23×3
Baking Dish	1 quart	1 L	—
or Casserole	1½ quart	1.5 L	—
	2 quart	2 L	—